fresh hope through

New Perspectives

30 days of readings

CWR Waverley Abbey House, Waverley Lane, Farnham, Surrey GU9 8EP

National Distributors

AUSTRALIA
Christian Marketing Pty Ltd.,
PO Box 519, Belmont, Victoria 3216
Tel: (052) 413 288

CANADA
CMC Distribution Ltd.,
PO Box 7000, Niagara on the Lake,
Ontario LOS 1J0
Tel: 1–800–325–1297

MALAYSIA
Salvation Book Centre (M),
Sdn. Bhd, 23 Jalan SS2/64,
Sea Park, 47300 Petaling Jaya, Selangor
Tel: (3) 7766411

NEW ZEALAND
Christian Marketing NZ Ltd,
Private Bag,
Havelock North
Tel: 0508 535659 (toll free)

NIGERIA
FBFM, Medium Housing Estate, Block 34, Flat 6,
Glover St., E.M., Lagos, PO Box 70952, Victoria Island
Tel: (01) 611160/866451

REPUBLIC OF IRELAND
Scripture Union
40 Talbot Street, Dublin 1
Tel: (01) 8363764

SINGAPORE
Campus Crusade Asia Ltd.,
315, Outram Road
06–08 Tan Boon Liat Building,
Singapore 0316
Tel; (65) 2223640

SOUTH AFRICA
Struik Christian Books (Pty Ltd)
PO Box 193, Maitland 7405,
Cape Town
Tel: (021) 551 5900

USA
CMC Distribution, PO Box 644,
Lewiston, New York 14092–0644
Tel: 1–800–325–1297

Breakthrough to Love. Copyright © 1996 by David and Maureen Brown
Published 1996 by CWR
Cover design: CWR Production
Design and typesetting: CWR Production
Printed in Great Britain by Wace Corporate Print, Poole
ISBN 1 85345 102 9

breakthrough to
LOVE

Building a Better Marriage

David and Maureen Brown

Biography

David and Maureen became Christians in 1973 through the break up of their own marriage. God restored this to them and in 1987 they began running marriage weekends within the church setting. David's career spans the motor industry and an international broadcasting company. He began working full time in the King's Church in Aldershot in 1983. Maureen has been a full-time housewife and mother to three children and they now have four grandchildren. As well as travelling abroad to such places as India and the USA with *The Marriage Agenda* they are kept very busy with the local branch of the King's Church in Cranleigh in Surrey.

God's
Intentions

"You have heard of the perseverance of Job and seen the purpose of the Lord – that the Lord is very compassionate and merciful."

James 5:11 (NKJ)

I f ever a man persevered it was Job. His life was surrounded by loss of loved ones and he lived from crisis to crisis. Even his friends did not comfort him. However, his trials brought about a transformation which at the end of his life found him with far more than when he started.

It may be that you, or a family friend, are at this moment going through a time of crisis in your marriage. Perhaps it seems that everything is falling down and this marriage seems more like a demolition site. However, even demolition sites are cleared and the land used to build something for a better use.

We once stood on a demolition site with rubble surrounding us and two small children wondering quite what was going on. That was just over twenty years ago and despite being counselled that, "you have nothing between you ... you should divorce", we responded to a different voice, the voice of the Good Shepherd. We did not know Him but He did keep calling until we individually accepted Him as Lord and Saviour of our lives.

That is when He stepped on to our "demolition site", cleared away the rubble and began to rebuild something better. It took time and some pain but we allowed Him to clear the site until new foundations could be put in and built upon.

Perhaps you are not looking at a demolition site but a crack or two in the fabric which could threaten the whole. If you have only a crack, do not patch over the affected area, but allow the Lord to cut back to the sound material and rebuild a better structure. Unless the foundation is secure, then a patched up crack will only crack further and the whole could collapse without warning.

In society we see many marriages failing, innocent victims of a battle started long ago by the father of lies (John 8:44). Even Christians get caught up in this battle and find themselves in the divorce courts. Let us pray for those who are hurting so much – divorce is not the second unforgivable sin. People need our love, not our condemnation.

To go against society's trends is not easy, but so worthwhile and perfectly "do-able." Looking back we would say that it was at times painful and we nearly failed again. We did have "down" times but we seem now only to have gained benefits. Our children have left home, married and have their own families. We can say, "Yes, it was worth it – thank you Jesus."

As we commence these days together let us encourage you in that if He can do it for us, He can, with your co-operation, do it for you.

For reflection and action:

❧ *Put on the armour of God (Ephesians 6:10–18) and stand daily.*

❧ *The armour and weapons are for fighting forwards. Our rear is protected – "And the God of Israel will be your rear guard" (Isaiah 52:12, NKJ).*

❧ *Find somewhere to be alone and pray: "Father I need my marriage to be what You have always wanted it to be. I pray for my husband/wife that together we will be open to You. I ask not for what we can get out of it – but for what You can put into us. Jesus, may Your light shine in us and build us upon You, the Rock, Amen."*

Beginning
a Foundation

"The foundations were laid
with large stones of good
quality ..."
1 Kings 7:10

Many of our majestic cathedrals are in need of expensive repair. Often the cause for this lies with the traffic passing close to the building. Not only do the exhaust fumes cause damage to the stonework, but the vibrations from the vehicles affect the very foundations. These move and create serious defects, even up into the roof line.

In this case an external force, the vehicle traffic, has created internal problems. Before any remedial work can be carried out an inspection and rectification of the foundations are called for.

So it is with marriage. Often external forces act upon our relationship, causing damage and lasting harm. Like the cathedral, we will need to look at the foundations of our marriage before attempting any rebuilding work.

It is interesting to note that when Jesus spoke of men building houses, He illustrated that the one which stood up against the storm was the one built upon the rock (Luke 6:48,49) and not sand. We have had couples come to us and, on the surface, have everything going for them: good house, car, careers, education, children etc., but are in a crisis. As we talk together, it becomes obvious that they are not standing on anything that is firm and solid. In fact they are swayed by outside influences – changes in interest rates, facing redundancy, health problems, etc. We can all face these whatever our income or lifestyle, for we all face the storms of everyday life.

It is not the pressure upon us that causes the damage, but what we are standing on – rock or sand? Are you standing upon the rock of Jesus? Is your marriage based upon God and His Holy Word? Ours wasn't, but when we moved from the sand to stand upon the Rock things changed.

We discovered that when Isaiah prophesied, *"Behold, I lay in Zion a stone for a foundation, a tried stone ... a sure foundation"* (Isaiah 28:16, NKJ) the words are as effective today as the day Jesus fulfilled them. The Hebrew words, *Yasad* and *Musad,* which are translated as 'foundation' in the above Scriptures, have in their meaning, 'large, heavy, solid.' They are used where what is to be built upon them is to endure and last for many generations. What you put down as a foundation into your marriage will affect not just you, but also your children and your children's children, and even their children.

For this use foundations are laid with care, precision and carefully chosen to withstand the pressures to be inflicted upon them. Within marriage we equally need to lay a quality foundation with care. This is what we aim to do in the next few days.

For reflection and action:

&❧ *Foundations can be beautiful and adorned. They can also reflect the beauty of the finished work.*

&❧ *Read and meditate on Revelation 21:18–21.*

Foundations
for a
Good
Relationship

"... The foundation was laid ..."

Zechariah 8:9

To build a good marriage relationship you have to have a good foundation. When we became Christians we had two new experiences to cope with, walking with the Lord and walking with each other in a new marriage. There were trials and tribulations along the way, but the foundations we received were not like the foundations of a house, but more like the foundations of a road, perhaps like an old Roman road, whose strong stones we could walk along.

Among the first actions you will need to take to lay these foundations will be to recognise the need to say sorry and to ask each other's forgiveness for past hurts which you have probably inflicted upon one another. All the old rubbish that has been put in the dustbin with the lid jammed firmly on, has to be taken out and dealt with. Learn to communicate, to talk to each other, to express your feelings to each other. Feelings are neither right or wrong. If you feel hurt or even just put out by something that has been said, or the way in which it was said, say so. It is so easy to assume that the other one knows exactly how you are feeling and what you are thinking.

We cannot emphasise enough that if issues do come between you, to share them, talk them through as a matter of priority, no matter how big or small, or how silly they may seem. Work them through together to resolve them. Doing this brings you closer to each other and pushes the enemy out. Send all thoughts of selfishness out of the window, you are in this together.

We had to learn to love and trust one another again.

Trust, once broken, takes time to rebuild, and without trust it is very difficult to build. Trust and friendship go hand in hand and marriage needs to have both these ingredients. Basically, we were good friends and enjoyed doing similar things, but we had to learn to build on that friendship.

By giving love away (to your spouse) you will receive it back in full measure, pressed down and overflowing (Luke 6:38). The Bible says *"Cast your bread upon the waters"* (Ecclesiastes 11:1), and if you cast your love upon your spouse, it will come back to you. Loving your partner is wanting the very best for them, as God wants the very best for you.

Unless you are looking for a miracle, it will take time to build and building is a gradual process. Learn to stand upon the Rock and trust, not only each other, but also God in all of this. Know that what you want for yourselves and your children, God wants for you even more and has only your highest interests at heart. The benefits far outweigh the cost.

For reflection and action:

❧ *With the help of the Holy Spirit, reflect on how you may have hurt your spouse in some way, whether in word or deed, and consider the way in which you might say sorry.*

❧ *Matthew 5:9 – Jesus said, "Blessed are the peacemakers."*

❧ *Romans 3:23 says that "All have sinned and fall short of the glory of God."*

God's
Image

"Let us make man in our image,
in our likeness ... male and
female he created them."
Genesis 1:26,27

In the beginning God created and set in order the heavens, the earth and all its fullness. At the fresh dawn of creation God placed mankind in the centre of a self-sustaining world which would provide all that they would ever need. At the end of that sixth day of creation God said, having surveyed His work, *"It was very good"* (Genesis 1:31).

During this creative period, however, something did not quite fit perfectly the first time around. What was it? Examine Genesis 2:18 and you will discover that what was not good was that man should be alone. Man on his own would be in isolation, he would have no one to call upon that was like himself. God's answer? *"I will make him a helpmate"* (Jerusalem Bible). Someone to stand alongside.

That word "helpmate" (or helper, helpmeet etc.) describes what God wanted in His heart. Someone who would be there at man's side, a comforter, an encourager, a supporter. Someone who would help him face life. In this duality of male and female together mankind could rule, or have dominion, over what the earth produced (Genesis 1:28).

The meaning in the Hebrew here for "helpmate" or "helper" is so similar to the word used in John's Gospel when Jesus said to His disciples that if He did not go away the Helper (Counsellor) would not come (John 16:7). The Amplified Bible uses the words "comforter, strengthener, standby" and to be "in close fellowship with you" in its rendition of this verse. We like to feel that right back in Genesis God was laying out a pattern of care and companionship for man. Also that right at the beginning God was causing mankind to peer over the horizon to a better king, Jesus, and a better helper, the Holy Spirit.

In the beginning God caused man to have a wife (Genesis 2:24) and by so doing He would use this relationship, which we call marriage, to reflect His relationship with mankind. Later marriage would be used to reflect Jesus and His Bride the Church. However, in this dawn of creation Adam goes over to his helpmate and proclaims *"This is now bone of my bones and flesh of my flesh; she shall be called 'woman', for she was taken out of man"* (Genesis 2:23). While this is a good translation of the Hebrew, it does not quite convey the very thrust of the original meaning. The literal translation is more on the lines of "He went over to her and exclaimed 'wow!' "

May we ask, how is the "wow" in your life? Does she still "wow" you or do you still "wow" him?

For reflection and action:

❧ *Think how, in Scripture, God provides for people not to be alone – Elijah, Ruth, Esther are only three of many examples.*

❧ *Marriage is God's idea and design, for mankind's benefit, health, enjoyment and companionship. If you are not experiencing this, who has robbed you?*

Our
Image

"For our struggle is not against flesh and blood, but ... against the authorities ... powers ... spiritual forces of evil."

Ephesians 6:12

How many of us see ourselves as God sees us? Most of us have a damaged self-image in one form or another – like distorted mirrors in amusement parks. Where do we get this picture from? God says we are made in His image, which is good, so why do many of us persist in seeing ourselves in a poor likeness of God? Why do we have to grapple with this picture over and over again and whenever anyone says anything positive about us, we still have difficulty in believing it?

The image we have of ourselves is the reflective image that our parents, mostly unwittingly, gave to us. I, Maureen, was always told and grew up with the knowledge that my parents wanted a son (they were going to call him Kenneth). They never told me they were disappointed with me and, relatively speaking, I had a happy childhood. But unconsciously, my parents did not expect a lot from me, I was not quite what they were wanting. I was often compared with other children and also told, "What will people think of you?" I grew up with this awful picture of wondering what people thought of me, to the point of desperately wanting to gain people's approval.

Our youngest son once said to me that we had never really encouraged him and never believed he would do any good. I was astounded and shared this injustice, as I felt, with our eldest son. He, would you believe, agreed with our youngest son. Apparently the body language was coming over loud and strong and again, unwittingly, I had passed this poor self-image of myself on to our own children. Secretly I found it hard to believe that they could succeed, although I knew they were capable of it. Consequently they were not encouraged as they should have been.

As the above Scripture states, we are not struggling against flesh and blood, but against authorities and powers. The battle is in the dark recesses of our mind. So how do we overcome a poor self-image? By accepting what the Bible says about us, that we are made in God's image, not the image inflicted upon us. Sometimes it takes a long time to overcome these wrong perceptions, but husband and wife do need constantly to encourage and build each other up.

Husbands and wives need to be open to one another. 1 John 1:7 says we need to walk in the light with one another as He, Jesus, is in the light, so that His blood purifies us from all sin. We need constantly to build confidence, trust and faith in our spouse.

For reflection and action:

❧ *Remember that forgiveness is the key.*

❧ *Read and meditate on Psalm 37:1–6. Note that if we trust in the Lord (v. 3), delight in the Lord (v. 4), and commit our way to Him (v. 5), His reward is to make us "shine" etc (v. 6).*

Pushes
from the
Past

"For the good that I will to do, I do not do ..." Romans 7:19 (NKJ)

ow many of us at times get exasperated because what we try to do, we don't, especially in our marriage. Making matters worse, we then do the very thing we know we do not want to do! It seems that Paul also had this problem. In verse 20 of Romans 7 he finally concluded that this was due to the *"sin that dwells in me."* At least we are not alone in this.

Why do I so often do something that upsets my spouse when I know it will? Why do I behave in this way? Why am I like this when I am a Christian? Let us examine how the thief has already come to rob, kill and destroy (John 10:10).

Most of us have heard the phrase, "the sin of the fathers." The Hebrew word for sin here is *avon* which has in its meaning the very thing Paul was speaking of above. *Avon* appears 232 times in the Old Testament and on occasions is translated as "mischief". *"The mischief of the fathers ..."* gives a clearer picture. It is this that God says He will *"visit upon the third and fourth generations"* (Exodus 20:5). These words formed part of the Ten Commandments. Powerful stuff!

When I became a Christian I became a new person, all the old passed away. But while this is true, the "old man" in each of us does have a habit of coming through at times. This has to be seen in the context of Paul's letter to a church which was not exactly perfect, yet. Bible commentators suggest that this new nature has to be *cultivated* by spiritual decisiveness to grow in Christ and not reverting to putting on the *old suit* of the former life.

We are all the product of our past. Our early life is

cradled in our parents and school etc., who while seeking the best for us, inflict wounds which they have no intention of doing. These hurt and damage us. At the time they are very real, but time passes and adulthood, courtship and marriage take us away from home and into a new family and lifestyle. But the scars are still there.

These "iniquities" go back to our great great grandfathers. Four generations and thirty people in both husband's and wife's family line. Any iniquity (or mischief) will affect us. Maureen illustrated yesterday how her parents' comments had been passed on to our children. Her parents, like ourselves, were responding to hurts, scars and bruises in their lives. They, like us, did the best they could in the circumstances.

As we looked at our families some while ago we began to see other "iniquities" in past generations. The phrase, "an accident looking for somewhere to happen" was true in our case, but we came to appreciate why it went wrong. In every step each parent was trying to do the best they could and, therefore, blame could and should not be put on anyone. Blame achieves nothing, only forgiveness can.

For reflection and action:

❧ *Before we move onto the way to overcome them, it may be good to look at some of the iniquities in your family.*

❧ *Whatever things are: True, noble, just, pure, lovely, of good report, virtue and praiseworthy: think on these things (Philippians 4:8).*

Annulled

"And the Lord has laid on him the iniquity of us all"
Isaiah 53:6

In his fifth sermon, running from chapter 52:13 through to 53:12, Isaiah prophesies much that Jesus would accomplish on the cross centuries later. In these few verses the very life-work of the Saviour is concisely set out.

As Christians we quote, *"By his wounds you have been healed"* (1 Peter 2:24) when we are sick. Peter was himself quoting what Isaiah wrote in verse 5 of the passage above. Isaiah was looking to a future event, Peter was looking back at the fulfilment and present availability of this accomplishment. So can we.

Many of the words contained in this section of Isaiah are so well known to us, *"We all, like sheep, have gone astray"* etc. Is it because they are so well known that we overlook their truth and power? David remembers vividly as a young boy singing Handel's *Messiah* in the school choir. At the time the words meant nothing, to him it was the singing and not the song. But when he became a Christian it was the song that held his attention. Even today he can clearly recall the problems in rehearsals over this passage from Isaiah 53:4ff. Perhaps this is why this piece of Scripture is firmly set in his memory.

We were reading through this passage a few years ago as our marriage was being rebuilt and something leapt from the page. Like Paul we struggled with those things we spoke of yesterday. While the Living and Revised English Bible translate verse 6 as "guilt", all other translations we have to hand use that word "iniquity" (again). So what struck us? Quite simply, in the fifteen verses of the sermon, where so much is mentioned, Isaiah prophesies no less than three times that Jesus' death would free us from the "iniquities" around our lives.

Take a look! Verse 5 says that He (Jesus) was *"crushed"* for our iniquities. Verse 10 says the Lord was pleased to crush Him. Verse 6 states that the Lord has laid the iniquity of us all on Him. Finally, in verse 11 we read that Jesus would justify many, as *"he will bear their iniquities."*

Three times in this short passage of Christ's accomplishment we are forcefully shown that these "pushes from the past", to quote Selwyn Hughes, would be dealt with – annulled – on the cross. *"It is finished"*.

For reflection and action:

۶ Lay aside these notes, pick up your Bible and read Isaiah 53.

۶ Allow God's Word to penetrate you.

۶ Meditate upon His Word.

۶ Compare Isaiah 61:1, "Freedom for the captives" with Luke 4:18,19 and Jesus' statement, "Today this scripture is fulfilled in your hearing" (Luke 4:21).

۶ Thank God for a way out.

Put
Away

"For my strength comes to perfection where there is weakness." 2 Corinthians 12:9 (New Berkley Version)

So how do we deal with these pushes from the past? Paul says: "but when I became a man, I put away childish things" (1 Corinthians 13:11, NKJ). To quote Selwyn Hughes: "The Greek word for 'put away' is an extremely strong word. It means 'to put away, to break a hold, finish it off, have done with, render inoperative'. Childhood agendas don't just fall away like the leaves fall off the trees in the autumn; we have to 'put them away', have done with and be finished with childish things. If God highlights any of these things, bring them to Him and lay them at His feet. Decide to have done with them. Get out of the passenger seat and into the driving seat. Remember with God, all things are possible."

You will note that it is a question of our "putting them away": recognising these iniquities in our lives, and with the help and co-operation of the Holy Spirit and our will, turning them over to God in prayer and laying them on the altar. As Selwyn Hughes says, "We can get into the driving seat and have authority in our own lives." Sometimes we give the devil too much credit in our lives. 1 Corinthians 13:6 (NKJ) says that love *"does not rejoice in iniquity, but rejoices in the truth".* It is the *truth* that has set us free. Therefore, for us to hold on to, or dwell in, our iniquities or unrighteousness is not rejoicing in the truth, because it is the truth that has set us free. Jesus is the truth. Hallelujah!

Unfortunately, we all have had hurt in our lives, intentional and unintentional, and quite often that hurt seems to stick to us like glue and can rise up in us again. Scars can take a long time to heal over. But the

Lord has provided a way for us and that way is forgiveness. Forgiveness is the key, but freedom from hurt does not necessarily come instantaneously. Quite often it is a process, a way of living. Someone has said: "The first mark of maturity is this: the willingness to accept the responsibility for being what we are. There can be no denial of the fact that our surroundings, our upbringing, our environment, bring strong influences to bear upon us, but it is only those parts to which we respond that influence us. We do the responding. The choice is always ours."

In Matthew 6:6 it says: *"But when you pray, go into your room, close the door and pray to your Father, who is unseen. Then your Father, who sees what is done in secret, will reward you."* Sometimes our hurts are so deep they can only be shared with the One who knows all our secrets and who knows where our innermost hurts and fears lay buried.

For reflection and action:

❧ *Take time out to go into your inner room and lay these hurts and fears at His feet.*

❧ *Have done with these things, Jesus came to set you free.*

Accepted

"... by which he has made us accepted in the Beloved."

Ephesians 1:6 (NKJ)

Before we move onto another part of marriage, we are very aware that there are those who have deeper scars in their lives than those we have covered. For some, families have come well away from God's ideal for them and the opposite of love is more normal.

We were both born in the early part of World War Two and grew up in London. Many of our friends lost not only fathers away on active service, but also parents and loved ones from enemy action from the skies above. The pain for some of these still lingers on in their lives today.

Sadly, some families seem to live almost in a war zone. Externally it can look okay, but internally a battle is often going on. There are those who, through no fault of their own, have been caught up and carry the scars, which may not be obvious on the outside, but within are very real. The scars are those of abuse within the family. Scars of emotional, mental, physical or sexual origin; scars that never have had time to heal and can make one feel unacceptable, dirty and lonely.

We do see couples who carry these scars within them. They can, and do, impact their marriage relationship. We cannot answer the question, "Why did X, Y, Z do this to me?" Often those who have perpetrated this evil do not know themselves. It has happened and is part of our fallen world, but we are not alone. Paul emphasises this in our opening Scripture. We are accepted by God with no strings attached. "Follow me" is all Jesus said to each of His disciples. No in-depth enquiry as to their life, background or abilities. Just, *"Follow me and I will make you fishers of men."*

God accepts you for who you are and what you can achieve in Him, not for what is in your background. *"For he foreordained us ... to be adopted ... as his children"* (Ephesians 1:5, Amplified).

Some can believe that He accepts us because of what they read in the Scriptures. Others may find that they need someone to guide them into freedom, perhaps through counselling. There are those within The Association of Christian Counsellors who are skilled and loving within this area. Some may find that one or more of the excellent Christian books now available do help in this area. Whichever method you decide upon let us encourage you to embark upon it, as your marriage will be enhanced by the benefits of release. Remember that you are accepted in Him.

For reflection and action:

🍂 *You are accepted in Christ.*

🍂 *Jesus proclaimed freedom to the prisoners (Luke 4:18,19).*

🍂 *Seek help, counsel and prayer.*

🍂 *Be open to your spouse.*

Not
a Contract

"... the wife of your marriage covenant." Malachi 2:14.

Whether you were married in church or a registry office, the words used during the ceremony are the same. In England and Wales there is a legal requirement that certain phrases are spoken and repeated. At the end of either ceremony the bride and groom and two witnesses sign a register book. When complete you are then legally married.

This can make the whole ceremony look more like a legal contract. This is more so when even the spot on which the wedding takes place is defined as the only place where a couple can legally marry. There are other legal requirements covering rights, approved persons for the ceremony, registered buildings, access of public and a certified person to make returns, among other things. We are handed a piece of paper that contains signatures after the wedding which is a certified copy of the entry into the Register. The state recognises this as the evidence that a couple are legally married. Thus all of this tends to reinforce the idea that we have entered into a contract.

However, in the verse above, contract is not mentioned. It refers instead to a marriage covenant, for marriage is a covenant and not a contract. The vows you took were not written down and signed, but were spoken out so all could hear. When God made a covenant with Moses or Abraham He did not get them to sign, with Him, a piece of legally binding paper. When Jesus opened the new covenant, He did not set out the terms and conditions which we had to sign.

In the instances above one aspect was used to signify the sealing of the covenant and that was blood. In the Old Testament it was the blood of bulls and lambs, in the New it was the very blood of Jesus. Where blood flows there will be a sacrifice, and a sacrifice has to be offered.

In marriage there is also a sacrifice that has to be made. Each has to lay down their own interests, personal items and self so that together something can grow. Marriages in crisis have often blurred the reality of this sacrificial lifestyle. We can so easily ask ourselves, "What is in this for me, what am I getting out of this?" rather than, "What can I give into this for us."

Self and selfishness has to be sacrificed. Without that sacrifice there can be no covenant. Without that covenant there can be no reflection of God's covenant with Israel and Jesus' covenant with His Bride, the Church.

For reflection and action:

🍃 *"For God so loved the world that He gave ..." (John 3:16)*

and

🍃 *"Whoever loses his life ... will find it" (Matthew 10:39).*

🍃 *Pray to be able to let go of self and take hold of "us".*

A Covenant

"According to the word that I covenanted with you ..."

Haggai 2:5 (NKJ)

In the Old Testament the Hebrew word for covenant is *berith* while in the New Testament it is the Greek word *diatheke.* However, in the verse above the word "covenant" is from two Hebrew words, *karoth berith,* which means "to cut a covenant". A literal translation would be: "According to the word when I cut the covenant with you".

In the Old Testament the sacrifice that was to be offered as a covenant offering was cut in two and those who offered it walked between the pieces (Jeremiah 34:18–20). In the New Testament it was the body of Jesus that was cut by the nails and the spear.

Recording artistes will talk about "cutting a disc" when making a record. When a new road or bridge is opened, often a tape will be cut to signify this. When a baby is born the umbilical cord is cut. Cutting does something.

In marriage there is the need to cut something, perhaps the ties with home. On a wedding day the symbols of cutting, sacrifice and covenant are there for all to see – if we look. As the bride walks down the aisle she symbolises the sacrifice both families have made in bringing up their children. The groom stands at the front awaiting his bride to symbolise the day Jesus will receive His Bride (Revelation 22:17). The groom stands away from his family to symbolise he has left his father and mother – a cutting away. The bride is given away, again to symbolise a leaving. Rings are exchanged to symbolise a joining together. Cutting of the wedding cake is to symbolise the cutting of a covenant. The toast symbolises that one day those of us who are in Christ will lift up the cup and drink of the new wine with Jesus in heaven (Matthew 26:29). There are many other symbols throughout the day.

In a marriage in which crisis is real enough we need to take time to reflect upon what we actually did on our wedding day. We were married because that was what we wanted and that was what couples did. We certainly did not think about our actions to any great extent, neither were these ever explained to us. We did not "cut" anything together.

Perhaps you were like us, not realising that when two agree anything before our Father in heaven, it is done for us. Our vows were made together and God took us seriously because He wanted to make us one flesh (Genesis 2:24).

For reflection and action:

❧ *Are you in a crisis because you have not realised what plans God had for you on your wedding day?*

❧ *Are you resisting God in your life or marriage?*

❧ *Ask God, in prayer, what plans He has for both of you.*

Day 12

Reflections

"Come ... I will show you ... the wife of the Lamb".

Revelation 21:9

We would like to help you understand that the day you got married you were not just entering into a contract with the person standing beside you, but were entering into a covenant relationship and that marriage is a covenant for life. It is not a contract that can be torn up when things aren't working out the way you would like.

A good way to describe the difference between a covenant and a contract is this:

1. A covenant is based on trust between parties. A contract is based on distrust.

2. A covenant is based on unlimited responsibility. A contract is based on limited liability.

3. A covenant cannot be broken if new circumstances occur. A contract can be made void by mutual consent.

As you can see a contract is a legal agreement, binding in law. It is written down and can be torn up if circumstances don't suit it anymore; whereas a covenant is more a joining of hearts by the spoken word; our vows can only be spoken.

In the context of marriage it is a question of sacrifice to each other, of dying to each other as a reflection of God sacrificing His only Son. The same relationship that God has with His Son, and that husband and wife have with each other, reflects the covenant relationship that God has with us, His Bride, the Church. It is the three-edged cord which is not easily broken, Father, Son and Holy Spirit – husband, wife and Jesus. All through the Bible, from the relationship that God had with Adam and Eve in Genesis to that of Jesus and

His Bride, the Church, in the book of Revelation.

God ordained marriage for the benefit of society and a place where children can grow up in security. Only when the marriage bond is held in honour is society healthy and whole. We are seeing the reverse of this today and we need to appreciate the benefits that God has placed in marriage for us. To Jews the home and family is central to their way of life and is a place where they can go and shut the door on the world. It is a place of security and something that has stood them in good stead down through the centuries.

How do the practical implications of being in a covenant relationship work out? It is all very well talking about it in a spiritual sense, but we have to work it out down here on earth in the nitty-gritty of our everyday relationships. Derek Prince has put it quite simply in his book *The Marriage Covenant*. It is a question of what can I give rather than what can I get. It is a question of giving and serving one another.

For reflection and action:

♣ *Examine the following aspects of covenant which the New Testament illustrates as the way Christians are to act towards one another:*

♣ *To wash one another's feet (John 13:14).*

♣ *To build up (or edify) one another (Romans 14:19).*

♣ *To accept one another (Romans 15:7).*

♣ *To comfort one another (1 Thessalonians 4:18, NKJ).*

♣ *To pray for one another (James 5:16).*

Grace

"I hate divorce ..." Malachi 2:16

Marriage is a covenant that God ordained to be for, *"as long as ye both shall live"*. Death of one of the spouses would be the only reason for remarriage. However, God recognised that man, once fallen, would not always find the best He had in mind for him. Man would harden his heart to God, marriages would fail and divorce would occur. Moses brought the law in on divorce which the Jews questioned Jesus on in His day.

Divorce is not God's best for us, but divorce does occur, and those who go through this trauma often feel guilty over what has happened. Many who are facing a crisis in their marriage, whether the first or subsequent marriage, often struggle within themselves about Scriptures like the one above and the reality of the situation in which they find themselves.

Many great theologians and writers down through the centuries have argued over divorce, as to whether it is permissible to remarry or not. We do not wish to add to your struggle, but would say that there is only one unforgivable sin, and divorce is not it.

David Phypers in his book, *Christian Marriage in Crisis* sums it up well when he points to the aspect of grace. Grace has not been given so that we can do whatever we want to do – get divorced so that we can marry someone else – but given so that we can receive forgiveness for what we have done. Dietrich Bonhoeffer in his book *The Cost of Discipleship* has referred to this type of thing as "cheap grace" within the Church. When we repent of those actions, grace can flow into us and rebuild the dry and barren places.

Within the UK, statistics show that second marriages show a much higher failure rate than first marriages. This is probably why God said that He hates divorce, because He knew the dangers that could follow. But even here grace can bring about a change.

We have come across ministers who have applied the "Law" when faced with marriages in crisis, sending wives back to be beaten, and allowing their husband's adultery and other abuses. They needed to apply grace. If any wife, husband or children are in danger, then there needs to be a separation. Separation gives space to look objectively into the situation and seek expert help. Separation is not divorce.

Why separation? So that grace can be allowed to enter in and do its work.

For reflection and action:

❧ *Grace has been described as **G**od's **R**iches **A**t **C**hrist's **E**xpense.*

❧ *"The Lord will give grace ... no good thing will he withhold ..." (Psalm 84:11, NKJ)*

❧ *By grace you have been saved (Ephesians 2:8).*

❧ *God gives grace to the humble (Proverbs 3:34).*

❧ *Grow in grace (2 Peter 3:18).*

Day 14

Balance

"Be subject to one another."

Ephesians 5:21 (NASB)

Marriage is a balance, how often have we heard that? The word "submit" is bandied about in the context of Christian marriage and often viewed askance by the world. But the Scripture quoted above quite clearly says we should be subject to one another out of reverence for Christ, or as the Phillips translation puts it, *"fit in with each other because of your common reverence for Christ."* Live considerately with one another, this makes for much more balance in your marriage.

The word "submit" is used in verse 24 of Ephesians 5, but it does not say "submit or else". Everything is in subjection to something else. We are subject to the laws of our Government (whether we like it or not). We are subject to the vagaries of the weather, we are subject to the rules of the company we work for, or are subject to the timetables on the railway. Whichever way you look at it, we are all subject in one way or another to something else. But if the subjection is righteous then the subjection works for our protection, and so it is in the Ephesians 5 Scripture. Women are subject to their husbands, but husbands are subject to Christ. Which carries with it the greater responsibility?

Women are not doormats to be trodden on, or just the weaker vessel, but are equal heirs (1 Peter 3:7). Women's inheritance is the same. Women have equal treatment in the kingdom of God (quite unheard of in other religions). In Genesis 3:16 it says that men are called to "rule", and in 1 Timothy 3:5 the Phillips translation states, *"He must have proper authority in his own household, and be able to control and com-*

mand the respect of his children." Yet another translation says that a man needs to "rule" his own household literally meaning to "guide" or "lead the way". The responsibility is placed squarely on the shoulders of the husband, but it is vital the wife plays her God-given role. For when wives submit to their husbands and husbands submit to Christ the law of love begins to fall into place.

This, in today's world, sounds very old-fashioned, out of date and out of touch with society, but the world isn't making a very good job of it either, with marriage breakdown reaching an all-time high, teenage pregnancies, fatherless sons and daughters, and men who don't know how to be fathers because their role has been gradually eroded. Laws are there for our protection, not for destroying us, as society seems to be bent on doing.

Men and women are different, opposite, equal, essential to each other, but they are there to balance each other and bring balance to their family and society. Although their roles are different, it is absolutely vital that each has a part to play and each plays their part.

For reflection and action:

❧ *Read Ephesians 5:21. Be subject to one another out of reverence to Christ.*

❧ *Wives read: Ephesians 5:22–24 (Amplified).*

❧ *Husbands read: Ephesians 5:25–31 (Amplified).*

❧ *Both read: Ephesians 5:33 (Amplified).*

Differing
Roles

"... the wife must respect her
husband." Ephesians 5:33

The husband's role is to love his wife, but the wife's role is to respect her husband. Husband love, wife respect, or to put it another way, the husband is called to cover his wife and the wife to support her husband. Behind every great man is a great woman! Examine history to see this amply illustrated.

Wife, is your role very much like that, or are you kicking against it because of outside pressure and afraid of being seen as going against the flow? Perhaps it is in our nature as a woman for some of us to be more submissive than others, "responders" rather than "initiators". But we are still individual people – able to speak for ourselves. We have special talents, our own ideas, own interests, our own likes and dislikes and, of course, we are equal heirs in the grace of God (1 Peter 3:7).

A happy marriage is usually one which is balanced. Uneven marriages don't work. If they are all submission or all authority, the scales are weighted against them. Wives are a balance to their husbands, to complement them, recognising their authority in God, but also recognising it is in God's order of things, and remembering that in this order comes his responsibility before God for his actions. The dictionary definition of complement means "completeness" or "perfection", which is something for us to aim at and to try and achieve within our marriage.

Men are harder and stronger than women, physically and emotionally; they are not so easily hurt. For instance, if you see a man with a black eye you will wonder what he has been up to, but if you see a woman with a black eye it somehow seems more seri-ous, there is a pull at your heart strings. As we know, the Bible tells us that woman came out of man, God took a rib out of Adam's side and made Eve, and according to Matthew Henry's Commentary, women are more vulnerable than men, they need to be treat-ed with more care: "Woman was ... not made out of his head to rule over him, nor out of his feet to be tram-pled upon by him, but out of his side to be equal with him, under his arm to be protected, and near his heart to be beloved." In *The Message*, a recent version of the Bible, it puts 1 Peter 3:7 like this: *"Likewise you hus-bands live considerately with your wives as they lack some of your advantages."* The Bible illustrates that woman was the final creative act of God, with her He finished and said it "was very good" (Genesis 1:31).

Marriage is a partnership between equals, with different roles to play. But each role needs the other. Perhaps a bit like an aeroplane – the wings keep it up and the tail keeps it in a straight line. Lose one and something serious happens.

For reflection and action:

❧ *How can we each play our own role in marriage to glorify God that others might see the light of Christ?*

Day 16
Respect

"However, each one of you also must love his wife as he loves himself, and the wife must respect her husband."
Ephesians 5:33.

Ephesians talks a lot about submitting but what about respect? Wives can feel that not all husbands are worthy of respect, but the Bible calls us to respect them. Not to talk behind his back, or to run him down in front of others – "my husband can't even mend a fuse", or "he is useless at ..." Lack of respect can spread like a cancer, eating away at a marriage if not checked in time.

The word "respect" is not in fashion. One has only to look at the business world where first names are the in thing, and from dentists to hairdressers first names are now the norm. This is a trend which can eat away at respect, but the Bible calls us to respect our husbands. This is not always easy and some people tend to earn our respect naturally more than others. But respect can and has to be learnt. If a wife does not respect her husband, can the children be expected to respect their parents?

Learning to respect your husband is really learning to trust in God, to trust God in your husband. We can't change our husbands, only God can do that, but we trust that God will mould him into the man that He (and you) want him to be, if only we play our part.

We are called to be godly women, living according to what the Bible says about our role and seeking to hand down godly insights and Christian values to our children. As someone has said, if we don't hand these values down to our children then don't be fooled, we are just rearing pagans.

There is no substitute for a balanced family life. Families are the bedrock of our society and society is strong only when marriage and families are held in honour. One does not have to look far into society to see that the reverse of this is happening today.

Spend time together, say at least one evening a week as a family; eat a meal together; turn the television off, play a board game, go for a swimming evening, a walk or cycle ride, or just go fly a kite. Children will remember these family values you put into them, which they in turn will pass on to their children.

There are various stages in your marriage: just the two of you (the reason you were married in the first place). Then the babies come along ... all those night feeds! Life continually spent with the children (will we ever be on our own again?). Driving them here to a party, there to a sports event, parent/teacher evenings, continually driving. Then the first one leaves – to go to college or get married. Then another one goes and husband and wife possibly find themselves on their own again, wondering where all those years went, hopefully, knowing that they have done their job to the best of their ability. Marriage and bringing up children calls for continual changes in our relationship. Who said you married and then settled down!

For reflection and action:

❧ *What are the values you want to put into your children and how do you best go about doing it? Share and talk about these things.*

Blocks

"Walk in the light, as he is in the light." 1 John 1:7

In a marriage in crisis where do the problems stem from? Over the next few days let us examine these together, starting with the biggest, *communication.* In any verbal communication there are six possible messages:

1. What you mean to say.
2. What you actually say.
3. What the other person hears.
4. What the other person thinks he/she hears.
5. What the other person says about what you said.
6. What you think the other person said about what you said.

All you actually said was, "Good morning" or "How are you?" Prince Philip has been quoted as saying: "I know you believe you understand what you think I said, but I am not sure you realise that what you heard is not what I said." He has also been credited with the quote, "The inevitable consequences of more communication is a vastly increased area of misunderstanding." This is true and not just within marriage.

Many marriages are probably like the previous two quotes, but in Isaiah 2:5 it says, *"Come ... let us walk in the light of the Lord."* There is nothing as difficult as good transparent communication. All marriages come into conflict, undergo stresses and strains, but it is how we deal with these particular situations. Essentially marriages break down because of lack of communication and our lack of desire or inability to express exactly how we feel about any given situation. Somebody has said, nothing is as easy as talking; but nothing is as difficult as transparent communication.

Speaking involves listening and there are many blocks to communication:

There is the "too busy" block. "We will talk about it later, I want to watch this programme on the television." Or there is the "change the subject" block. One or other tries to talk about a particular subject but the other one is just not interested and talks about something completely different. Then there is the "defensive" block. "Why should I be interested in what you are saying, you don't exactly pay a lot of attention when I am talking." There is also the "guilt" block. "I really feel guilty about this situation so would rather not talk about it", commonly known as a "push it under the carpet" block or "put it behind the clock" block. There is also the "peace at any price" or "quiet life" block. The "false humility" block or the "rejection of feelings" block, and many more.

The basic reason behind these blocks is selfishness. We need constantly to pray and ask of the Lord the prayer of David: *"Search me, O God, and know my heart; test me and know my anxious thoughts. See if there is any offensive way in me ..."* (Psalm 139:23).

For reflection and action:

🍃 *Read and meditate on Psalm 139:23,24.*

🍃 *Ask yourselves – Do I/we hide behind "blocks"?*

🍃 *Each ask God to search your heart for your selfishness – not your spouse's.*

Day 18

Communication

"Speak to one another ..."

Ephesians 5:19

Marriage is a reflection of Christ's love for His bride – the Church – you and me. If we look at the life of Christ, we will see that often He spoke to His Father in prayer and He listened to His Father's voice. Put very simply He and His Father were in communication, they were on speaking terms, as it were.

Marriages that are facing a crisis nearly always demonstrate a failing in the area of communication. Listening to a speaker from Worldwide Marriage Encounter a few years ago we were not too surprised to learn that, in their experience, 95% of all marriage problems stem from the area of communication problems.

Despite, or may be because of, the plethora of communication styles now available to us, we still find it difficult to communicate. We can talk to each other using various forms, but that does not mean we communicate. It does not mean that we are getting across to our spouse what we are trying to say. Often one or other of the spouses is unable, or unwilling, to allow their thoughts or feelings to be expressed – maybe because in the past these have not been understood or accepted. But this does not mean we should give up and not try again.

Moses, on his initial meeting with God at the burning bush, raised all sorts of reasons why he would not be any good for the role God wanted for him – "Who has sent me?" ..."Who am I? ..." "No one will believe me!" ... "I am slow of speech!" (Exodus Chapters 3 and 4). But God had chosen him and did equip him to communicate His plans to His people.

Jesus has chosen you and will cause you to bear fruit and be able to communicate (John 15:16). Communication, like all life's skills, does have to be learnt and developed. It is not impossible to learn, even afresh, the art of communication to the one you love, your spouse.

In our efforts to learn, or relearn, the art of communication, let us consider the essentials of a simple telephone call:

1. There is something to communicate.

2. There has to be a desire to communicate.

3. Someone has to make the first move and pick up the telephone and dial.

4. The line must be open – not engaged.

5. The other person must answer.

6. It is a two-way line.

For reflection and action:

❧ *To help you begin to communicate on that "something" in 1. above, you may find the following question a useful tool to open the door: Tell me five things that I do that say, "I love you".*

Fathers

"Fathers, do not exasperate your children." Ephesians 6:4

Looking around our churches we see that in most, but not all, women out-number men. In our society, with so many single parent families, we see many wives and mothers having to take all the responsibility of raising a family.

One of the fears expressed to us by wives who face crisis in their marriage is the whole question of looking after their children on their own. The laws of our country tend to favour the mother in the child care area, rather than the father. It is rare for a father to gain custody. Yet children need a father and a mother.

Look at any magazine rack in any newsagent and you will discover many periodicals for mothers, mothers to be, motherhood etc. Their needs are catered for – but look for a magazine for fathers and you will almost certainly not find one. Men's magazines are confined to the top shelf type or sports. But men need the skills to father and be a father to their children.

In a marriage in crisis we have often discovered that within either or both spouses lies a lack of a father, or a bad father. They have been told to honour their father and mother, yet have been exasperated. Many women struggle with the father figure of God because of their own damaged father relationship. Men, especially young men, can react in violent ways due to this same damaged relationship. In her book *Farewell to the Family?* (IEA Health and Welfare Unit) Patricia Morgan points to the danger to our society of these unattached and predatory males.

Usually, but not always, a damaged father relationship can cause stresses even within a good marriage. Often these do not seem to be directly related. The devil, once he has damaged a life, does not point to the source of his infliction, but rather allures us to something else that looks to be the "obvious" reason. Do not be fooled, but rather seek freedom through Christ and, perhaps, seek the wisdom and guidance of a fellow believer to help you through.

For reflection and action:

❧ *Jesus came to "bind up the broken-hearted" (Isaiah 61:1).*

❧ *God the Father so loved you that He sent His only Son for you so that He would proclaim liberty to the captives and opening of the prison (John 3:16; Isaiah 61:1).*

❧ *You are no longer a slave but a son or daughter who through the Spirit of God's Son can cry out, "Abba, Father" or "Father, Father" (Galatians 4:6,7).*

❧ *Sit down before God, reach out in the Holy Spirit and pray, "Father show me, gently, what your fatherhood can be. I allow you to begin your healing process in me from today. Amen."*

Endure

"Our Father in heaven ..."

Matthew 6:9

Let us spend another day examining the role of a father. Within marriage the product of our love, our children, while a blessing, can often cause problems. Having reared three children ourselves through adolescence and into marriage, we would not like to say as to who has the most scars – them or us!

Children can, and do, come between mum and dad. They often seem skilled in this, picking up the rudiments in early childhood and developing these into what can be a very damaging tool later in life. That is, if they are allowed to. That is, if we do not discipline them.

Some marriages which are in crisis are being rocked simply over the matter of discipline. The word "discipline" often has the wrong connotation for many, being heavily handed out to – or by – us. But "discipline" comes from the word "disciple" which means "to copy someone", "to imitate someone's lifestyle", "to follow someone's teaching". Is that not what we want for our children? To follow us.

Discipline within the family is the responsibility of the father, of which there is no doubt. This does not mean he has to carry it all out, rather he takes responsibility for it. For that responsibility is shared with his wife. They need to discuss the various needs of each child, and the family as a whole – together. This need of discipline will change as the children get older and thus discipline will have to be flexible to accommodate this. It still needs to be done together though.

When children can see that by going to one parent rather than the other they can get exactly what they want, then the crisis within that marriage is very evident. It is already causing damage and needs serious addressing.

The above is even more important when a second marriage is entered into with both new spouses bringing with them their own children. The time to deal with this is *before* marriage, but if you are in this situation in marriage it does require both of you to sit down together and talk through the situation. Be careful not to throw words like, "They are your children" into your, possibly, already heated situation.

Wherever possible seek to discuss discipline away from the children's hearing and also be prepared to give more than a single occasion to talk through to a workable conclusion. It may seem obvious, but do pray before and after your discussion. If you do not come to any firm conclusion at first do not worry, give time for God to answer your prayers, remembering that if we cast our bread upon the waters, it will return to us after not many days (Ecclesiastes 11:1).

Love does endure all things (1 Corinthians 13:7). Often in any marriage, let alone one that is already in crisis, all we can do is to endure – especially so with respect to children.

For reflection and action:

❧ *Read 1 Corinthians 13:4–8 and look for how many of the attributes of love you can apply to your family.*

❧ *Determine to bear one another's burdens (Galatians 6:2) in the area of discipline of the children.*

Being a
Dad

"We cry out with deep emotion
Abba, namely, Father."
Romans 8:15, (Wuest expanded
translation)

Vine, in his *Expository Dictionary*, states that "Abba" is the word framed by the lips of infants and betokens unreasoning trust. "Father" expresses an intelligent appreciation of the relationship. The two together express the love and intelligent confidence of the child. Dads, we share the following with you to help you to this goal.

1. Be a guide. 1 Timothy 3:4 says: *"He [the father/ husband] must manage his own family well."* Often "rule" replaces "manage". This appears hard on the surface, but the original Greek infers a "guiding" of his household. Rather like a guide leads explorers through unknown and dangerous terrain to safety. Guide your children through life.

2. Be real – you are not perfect yet! Never be a perfectionist. Your children will never be exactly what you want them to be. With your loving care they can become who they really are, and with your loving prayer they can become who they are in God.

3. Be a brick! Not in a wall but as in a bridge – loving and communicating, accepting and receiving them as they are. Laying down your life so that they can build a better one. Become the good foundation for their lives

4. Do not stand in their way – rather play with them, allow them to touch and play with you. Have fun together. At eighteen months it might be building blocks, at eighteen years it might be under the car. Both require you to be at their level, together.

5. Be a listener. The real art of communication is to be a listener. Listen to your children and hear what

they are really trying to say – their fears, concerns, hurts, joys etc. This does not always require a verbal response – sometimes a hug is all that is required. Hearing is one thing, but listening will build an understanding with them.

6. Be worth looking up to. It is not good to instruct your children to tidy up or help Mum with the dishes if you don't do this yourself. Lead the way on morals, ethics, prayer etc. Do not have certain newspapers in the house – or eighteen-rated videos. Share with your children why.

7. Simply be in love with their Mum. Show affection to her in front of the children. Never be negative about her, argue or fight in front of the children, or within their hearing. However, never allow the fruit of your love, your children, to come between you.

Fathers, the world and our families are crying out for you to take on the responsibilities of fatherhood. Children in society are crying out for good fathers, wives are crying out for good husbands. It's time for men to take up their role again and Dads, when you have worked through the above you are ready for the next step – being a Granddad!

For reflection and action:

🍃 Wives, pray for your husbands every day.

🍃 Husbands, pray – "Father I need to learn of your Abba Father love for my children and reflect this to them. Help me and train me in this for their benefit and your glory and honour. Amen."

🍃 Further recommended reading, The Sixty Minute Father by Rob Parsons.

Day 22

Yoke or Blessing

"Craving wealth and resorting to ignoble and dishonest methods of getting it."

1 Timothy 3:8

(Amplified)

Finances do play a major part in our lives. Whether rich or poor, marriages in crises often display difficulties in the financial realm. Perhaps the crisis has come about because of financial problems, or because of the crisis we have tried to spend our way out and now have financial problems.

An accountant friend once told us that Jesus talked on the subject of money more than any other. Certainly Jesus, along with the rest of the Bible, draws our attention often to the use and misuse of money. The Bible says that the love of money is a root of all evil – not money itself.

How we obtain our income is important. Shady deals, under-the-counter transactions, or handling "hot" money will introduce tension in any couple. Matthew was a shady tax-gatherer before he became a disciple of Jesus. Zacchaeus was similarly employed and upon becoming a follower of Jesus offered to pay back fourfold what he had questionably received (Luke 19:1–10). Our income has to be as open as our lives. Personally, we would say never a "yours" and "mine" bank account, but rather an "ours" account.

What we do with our income is also important. The 10/80/10 principle is worth following. 10% of what enters your home should be given away. As Christians our 10% should be our tithe to our local church. 80% should be used to cover our household expenses (food, heating, clothing, rent/mortgage etc.) and 10% saved. If we have any excess in the middle 80% consider giving this as an offering somewhere.

That initial 10% (plus offerings) is a place in the Bible where God says we can rob Him, and that same 10% is the only place in the Bible where God says to us to prove Him in that He will pour out a blessing so much that we cannot hold it all (Malachi 3:8–11).

Put simply, be good stewards of your money. Give away what is God's and allow your finances to be a communication tool and not a shackle that binds you.

For reflection and action:

🙶 *Malachi 3:8–11. When we rob God of His tithes and offerings, we also deprive ourselves of blessings.*

🙶 *Matthew 28:11–15. Bribery leads to lies which have to be maintained at any cost.*

🙶 *2 Kings 5:20–27. Deception and lies always lead to a downfall.*

🙶 *Luke 16:11. By being righteous with money God will entrust us with His true riches.*

🙶 *1 Timothy 6:7. We cannot take our worldly possessions with us to eternity.*

🙶 *Luke 6:38. God's measures are fair, just and extravagant.*

🙶 *Pray: "Father help us to be good stewards of our income and to trust You in what is righteously yours. Amen."*

Pray

"Pray at all times with every kind of spiritual prayer keeping alert and persistent."

Ephesians 6:18 (Phillips)

Most people in a crisis or a jam, pray. Many of us find that prayer does not come naturally, it is difficult, not easy to find the time, one hundred and one reasons why we haven't got time to pray, so many things to do in our busy lives. And yet, if one finds oneself in a difficult situation, prayer doesn't take time, it just happens, it is an instantaneous response. Even people who don't profess to know God can find themselves praying, given the "wrong" kind of situation.

However, prayer for marriage and in marriage requires a different response, it takes time and effort and needs to be a specific act. It can be a sacrifice to set time aside to pray, and yet if we look at the Scripture quoted above, it says that we should use every kind of spiritual prayer, be alert and persistent in our praying. Prayer never ceases, it is a continual process.

Within a marriage it is vital that husband and wife pray together, for there is real strength in such prayer. It welds a husband and wife together.

A recent survey found that one in three marriages end in divorce, but if the couple were married in church and attended church regularly, the divorce rate fell to one in fifty. However, the survey also found that if the couple prayed together, the divorce rate fell to one in one thousand one hundred and five. The old adage, a couple who pray together stay together, obviously still holds good today.

Even so, to find time to pray together is not always easy and the devil will always seek to rob us of this.

When our children were young we found the best time to pray was in the evening, when they had gone to bed, but, of course, as they got older this was not possible, so we switched the time to pray first thing in the morning. To pray and read the Word together leads to much more agreement in the marriage, and not only do you talk to God, but you talk to each other more. Always a bonus in any marriage situation.

If your marriage is going through a difficult time, perhaps you have an erring spouse, or maybe there are outside pressures upon your marriage, things beyond your control such as difficult teenage children, redundancy or business failing. Then what better can you do than to lay these at the feet of the Lord in prayer? Psalm 55:22 says, *"Cast your burden on the Lord (releasing the weight of it) and He will sustain you."* (Amplified). King David, in this Psalm, is crying out to the Lord because of the hurt he felt regarding a close companion and friend. There is a place for crying, not just speaking, from our hearts to the Lord, and our prayers should be childlike, simple and honest.

For reflection and action:

❧ *Read Psalm 55 and Proverbs 3:5.*

Day 24

Sanctified

"For the unbelieving husband/
wife has been sanctified ..."

1 Corinthians 7:14

"**Y**ou cannot possibly understand, my husband is not saved and I cannot pray with him", a young wife said to us recently. Praying with him was the one thing she most wanted. In a marriage where only one of the partners is a Christian a "pressure" to be saved can be exerted upon the unsaved half. While appreciating the young wife's views, we learnt that she had never asked him if she could pray with him, only assumed so. One thing that should never be done in marriage is to assume anything.

That word "sanctified" should adjust our view on the subject of "unsaved" spouses. They are not heathen, they actually are in close contact with someone of God's family – you. As such they do have privileges from this union. Also, if God has saved one half of this union, do you not think that He wants to bring the other half in as well? Are you two not one now? (Genesis 2:24; Ephesians 5:31). Peace and not war is what God is seeking for your union. In verse 15 of 1 Corinthians 7 Paul ends with the words, *"God has called us to live in peace"*, words we need to remind ourselves of daily and pray daily. *"And God's peace be yours, that tranquil state ..."* is how the Amplified Bible opens Philippians 4:7. Peace is a gift from God and can be applied into a marriage crisis.

So how can you help this person into the kingdom? How can you ease the pressure in your marriage? We share the following from lessons learnt.

1. You cannot save him/her. Only Jesus can save anyone and Jesus said that no one would go to Him unless the Father draws him (John 6:44). Therefore, pray to the Father to draw him/her to Jesus. Remember the Christian walk is not your responsibility, but rather your response to His ability (Selwyn Hughes).

2. Be patient. This may take time and it just may be that God is working within you through this situation. Be encouraged when men like Smith Wigglesworth and Fred Lemon were once themselves part of an "unsaved" union.

3. Be real. Peter, in the third chapter of his first letter, writes about husbands being won over not by talk, but by the purity and reverence of their wives. He also goes on to speak to husbands with a warning that unless they are considerate, understanding, cherishing etc. towards their wives, God will not listen to their prayers.

4. Have a vision. Without vision a people perish (Proverbs 29:18, AV). See your spouse as saved and part of the kingdom. David Pawson once told a true story of a neighbour becoming part of God's kingdom through David taking this approach. It started with talking together over the garden fence, through to coming to church and finally becoming a Christian. Do you "vision" your spouse being saved?

For reflection and action:

❧ *Pray, "Father I want to apply patience and vision into our marriage. I pray for my partner as to the richest way they may glorify You. Help me to see them as fully part of eternity with You. Amen."*

Anchor
in a Storm

"... my words will never pass away." Matthew 24:35

Jesus was addressing His disciples here not long before He was to face the cross. He had just finished telling them the parable of the fig tree and ended by saying that heaven and earth would pass away, but His words never would. It must have seemed a bit perplexing to them. The very ground on which they stood, the scenery all around and the sky above, which they would clearly see, was one day simply going to vanish. Yet the spoken word, which they could only hear and not see, would always remain.

What Jesus was saying was quite simply that all they could see would change and one day vanish. But the comfort, encouragement, direction and life changing words of Jesus would always be there. When storms, changes in government and social upheaval came, the very power of Jesus' words would be a rock in an ever-changing world.

Those in crisis in their marriage often look back to the way things were and wish it had never changed. Perhaps they even got married to keep things as they were. However, life is not like that, and neither is marriage, which has to change continually. If it doesn't, it will stagnate and die.

Marriage has to have something that acts as an anchor to prevent it being blown off course. So what is your anchor? House and mortgage? Over the past few years with property prices tumbling, this is not the secure investment it once was. Career? With mergers, bankruptcies and economic stagnation, this is not as secure as in days gone by. Financial investment? True, big money can be gained, but can also be lost by an event in some distant country affecting the market.

We need the above to help us through life, but as anchors they do seem to shift around from time to time. We cannot quite imagine the captain of the QE2 anchoring to something that could easily move about. He would need something that was embedded into solid rock as a foundation.

It is that kind of foundation that we need in our lives and marriage. The rock of the Word of God. It has never changed, it never will. The world changes around it, but it remains the same Word, with the same values and the same Teacher.

Is the Word of God, the Bible, your foundation? Or does it quietly gather dust on some book shelf? "The devil is not amused with a Bible that has been well used," may be a line from a Cliff Richard song, but it illustrates the truth. A marriage that is tied into the Bible as its foundation will not be blown about by winds of change.

For reflection and action:

❧ *Read and meditate upon 2 Timothy 3:16.*

❧ *Teaching, rebuking, correcting and training, are all contained between the covers of God's holy Word.*

Love

"Love each other ..." John 15:12

How we have taken that little word "love" and made it mean so many things in so many situations.

Love is not easy to describe and is not always easy to discern. In a world that talks about "falling in love" as something simple and natural, why is it that quite a few people either never seem to, or fall out of it so easily? One can fall down a hole in the ground but never fall out of that hole. Rather a decision has to be taken either to climb out, or for someone to lift you out. Falling also implies getting hurt, for rarely does anyone fall and not get hurt.

Love never implies hurt or pain, except in the loss of a loved one when the reality of that love comes to the fore in grief. If it appears that we are saying that you can be sure of genuine love only through grief, we are not, but it does illustrate a point. God so loved us that He gave Jesus to die for us. We love Him because of His death, the laying down of His life. Paul, in Ephesians 5:25, instructs husbands to love their wives as Jesus loved us. According to the tense used in the original Greek, husbands are told to be continuously in love with their wives as Christ is continuously in love with His church. A tall order when so many of us husbands have never been shown what love actually is.

Let us help you to unravel some of the "mystery" as Paul puts it in Ephesians 5:32. This is not the final discourse on love. Many books fill many libraries on the subject, and songs are written and sung every day just about love.

In the years before becoming a minister of the

gospel, David was employed in the broadcast supply industry. In his work environment he had to quickly learn about television and radio and a simple television colour picture is a good way of describing love.

A view entering a television camera is broken down into various pieces of information part of which concerns colour. This is broken down into its red, green and blue components (the three primary colours) and is transmitted to your television receiver. Your receiver receives the picture in black and white and mixes them with the primary colour information and then presents you with an exact colour representation of the view the camera is looking at.

Love has three primary components (to be discussed tomorrow) which have to be blended through the black and white of our lives to represent the full colour of God's love to us in our marriage. For only within marriage can this be fully reflected. Unlike our television, love cannot be switched on and off at will, for love, God's love, is ever "broadcast" to us. In marriage, even a marriage in crisis, love is there and we need to receive it and in full colour.

For reflection and action:

🕭 *Read Philippians 4:8 and "think", as instructed in this Scripture, of the positive points of love within your marriage – either now or in the past.*

🕭 *Allow God to rekindle the flame of love within both of you (Isaiah 42:3).*

To Show
Love

"... as I have loved you."

John 15:12

Yesterday we likened love to the primary colours contained in a television picture. Today we want to examine these "primary" colours, so that these can be combined within our marriage to give a full picture of love.

The first of these primary colours is perhaps the green – the Greek word *agape* – "to love". This is the love that loves the unlovable and the unloving. The love that is never emotional, but rather firm and foundational. This is the love that is self-giving and is not something that happens to us, but something we make happen. It is the love that Jesus showed on the cross. It is the type of love that Paul instructs husbands to show to their wives in Ephesians 5:25, 28 and 33.

The second is certainly the blue element, the *phileo* type of love in Greek. This is the type of love shown by, and to, friends. It is a side by side relationship, working together for a common, mutual goal, the love that brings about companionship and co-operation. All marriages have to grow into this type of relationship and is the element of love most often shown to those outside. It will almost certainly illustrate some element of romance within its make-up, for romance is vital within marriage. Romance does not end with courtship and is something most husbands have to learn to apply.

Thirdly, we arrive at the red element of our colour picture of love, the physical, sexual part of love. Here we need to look at a non-biblical word in Greek for love, *eros*. From this word we get the English word erotic, and how the devil has soured us to misapply this aspect of marriage. This beautiful part of our life is only healthy and beneficial when contained within marriage – outside it brings only death, disease and despair. It is inspired by the biological structure of human nature. In a good marriage a couple will love both romantically and erotically. We do not want to upset anyone's sensitivity, but why should we allow the twentieth century's so-called "entertainment" industry to present to us the wrong picture of what God intended to be contained within marriage? God invented the sexual side of marriage, not Hollywood! He designed its benefits for married couples. A sexual union will not make a life partner, however, a married life will produce a sexual partner for life. While important, the erotic side of love cannot sustain a marriage and will only be beneficial where the other two aspects of love are flowing with it.

Like our television picture, when all three components of love are flowing together we can see the full picture in all its depth and beauty. Each "colour" individually disappears and blends with its neighbours to present the full range of colours. Within love this is probably the Hebrew word *ahabah*, the full spectrum of God's love to us, and the full spectrum of love found within a family reflecting this to the world.

For reflection and action:

☙ *Prayerfully examine together the aspects of love illustrated above. Is there one or more that is more dominant – or not being shown? Discuss together.*

Two into
One

"... and they will become one

flesh." Genesis 2:24

Two becoming one – there's more to it than meets the eye! A man and woman coming into marriage usually have different expectations of marriage, especially in the realm of the physical. The husband will tend to look at the relationship from a purely physical one, whereas the wife will look at the relationship from a more emotional one. His senses will be set ablaze by what he sees, whereas her senses will be aroused by what she feels in her emotions. So how do these two become compatible? How do two become one?

When a man marries he "acquires" something, usually a house and mortgage, someone to cook the dinner and iron his shirts (if he is fortunate), someone to meet his physical needs. His role seems to be much more of a function. When a woman marries it is with her whole being, her whole emotion, a sense of being given. So here we have the physical coming to meet the mainly emotional. The woman wants to feel secure and loved for who she is and not just what she is.

A woman needs romance in her life and, most importantly, needs to feel cherished. Dr. James Dobson says that a husband can ignore the romantic needs of his wife only at enormous peril. She doesn't want to feel used at the end of a long and tiring day, especially if she is out to work all day, or has small children or, as happens these days, both. Romance needs to come into our lives and should start at breakfast, not last thing at night.

What is romance? Just a few words of a dictionary definition: imaginative, visionary, poetic, extravagant, fanciful, impractical, sentimental of conduct. It's the small things, not the big things.

Equally, if there are any unresolved issues between you these need to be put right, you can't be romantic to someone you are not talking to. There is still a need to keep communication open. The sexual act itself is not the important thing for a man and woman, the important thing is the intimacy of heart and mind which in true love should precede the act. In other words you cannot make love in a vacuum. Don't let marriage ruin your sex life rather, let it enhance it. The purpose of God's gift to us of marriage is that sex within that union is safe and secure whereas sex outside of marriage can and does lead ultimately to disaster one way or another.

Dietrich Bonhoeffer said, "Marriage is more than your love for each other ... in marriage you are a link in the chain of generations ... in your love you are placed at a post of responsibility ... your life is private, but marriage is a status, an office."

For reflection and action:

❦ *Take time out together, take time to recharge your marriage batteries, take time out to have fun, take time out for romance.*

A Building to Last

"The wife is part of her husband
as long as he lives."
1 Corinthians 7:39 (TLB)

The day we were married we probably spoke the phrase, "until death parts us" as part of our vows – words that take a moment to say and a lifetime to live out. When we married we intended it to last. (If we don't, this could well be the root cause of a current crisis.) However, we are now caught up, or have been, in our crisis and we wonder if this marriage will last.

That word "last" is a four letter word like "love" and we can use each letter to examine four aspects which, when applied, will produce a relationship that will last.

The first aspect is *"listening"*. Our bodies have been designed with two ears and one mouth, a design which speaks of the need to listen twice as long as we speak. We have said previously that one of the arts of communication is to listen. In the middle of a marriage crisis one of the spouses, usually the wife, exclaims "He/she will not listen to me!" Listening involves the whole body, not just the ears. Listening involves not just hearing words, but also the feelings of emotion and motivation behind those words. Body language plays a major part. As walking away from the someone who is talking shows lack of interest, so moving towards shows we are interested in what we are hearing.

The second aspect is *"acceptance"*. One of the striking things of Jesus' life was His ability to accept people as they were. Acceptance in marriage is not taking something begrudgingly. It is to receive someone with all their faults as well as favours. Not one of us is perfect. We all have faults and we have to accept these. In marriage we have to accept our spouse's faults so that they can accept ours and can then feel accepted as a person for who they are, not for what we can get out of them.

Thirdly, there is the requirement to *"speak"*. Paul, in Ephesians 5:19, says, *"speak to one another."* To speak to one another implies looking at each other and not just mouthing words, but speaking from our hearts. Speaking should also build the other person up, never pull them down. Encouragement always seeks to build, and even in a crisis can restore a damaged relationship.

Finally, that little word *"Touch"*. Notice how Jesus would often touch someone, or allow them to touch Him. Touch conveys so much, either positive or negative. Many wives want their husbands to touch them, not in a way that is threatening, but rather a simple cuddle. Cuddling means protection and security for both of you. You both need that feeling of affection and protection cuddling will bring. It does reach heartfelt needs, even in the midst of a crisis.

For reflection and action:

❧ *The foregoing can be more simply expressed as:*

❧ *Listen – Keep open the lines of communication.*

❧ *Accept – Forgiveness is the key.*

❧ *Speak – Keep open the lines of communication – it is a two-way line.*

❧ *Touch – Affectionately.*

Twice the
Blessing

And the Lord restored Job's losses when he prayed for his friends ..." Job 42:10 (NKJ)

God responded to Job in a remarkable way. Firstly, He did not give back to Job what he had lost, but gave back double ..., *"Indeed the Lord gave Job twice as much ..."* verse 10 ends, a principle that Isaiah mentions in Isaiah 40:2, and Paul in 1 Timothy 5:17. In the parable of the sower Jesus expands this principle even further by stating that the yield to the seed sown in good soil would be thirtyfold, sixtyfold or one hundredfold. In this parable the end result was never nil.

Marriage is similar. If you put into it, you will get back double what you appear to have "lost". If you sow into it your result will be as the sower. Believe us, this has been our experience. The journey has not always been easy, but the goal is obtainable and the rewards beyond what we could ever imagine.

Secondly, Job prayed for his friends. We have mentioned before about prayer and friendship within marriage. Forgive us if we repeat ourselves, but prayer is as essential as oxygen is for life, and friendship is as vital in marriage as water is to sustaining life. If we are a disciple of Jesus then we are His friends and He laid down His life for us (John 15:13–15). Let us live our lives as husband and wife within this love, recognising the cost of that love to Jesus and ourselves.

We trust that you have benefited from reading this booklet, but do recognise that if your marriage was in crisis this is only a beginning. God does perform miracles in people's lives, but more often He performs healing – and healing can take time. God, we trust, has commenced a healing process in your lives. Allow

Him to continue for the rest of your lives together. As part of this continuous process we would encourage you to invest time on one of the many marriage refreshment weekends that CWR, ourselves and others within *Promoting Marriage* regularly run. It will be time well spent.

Today we would like to pray for you:

"Father, we pray for each couple who have read our words this month. We trust that they have heard You speak to them with words of love, comfort and healing. Whatever they have faced, may they know that You are ever ready to restore them to each other and to Yourself for Your glory. May they know of the hope of their calling in You. Amen."

For reflection and action:

Consider these questions together:

❧ *What are some of the things that I do that make you laugh?*

❧ *What do you remember as our greatest success?*

❧ *What is the hardest feeling for you to express? How can I help you express it?*

❧ *What do you think is the hardest feeling for me to express? How can you help me?*

❧ *What is the dream that you had about our marriage and family that has not been fulfilled yet? (Should you find yourself becoming negative, stop and reflect that you are building together – not tearing down.)*

❧ *There are things, good things, in your marriage. Dwell on these things (Philippians 4:8).*